Can You See What I See?

BIG BOOK OF SEARCH-AND-FIND FUN

by Walter Wick

CARTWHEEL BOOKS

AN IMPRINT OF SCHOLASTIC INC.

A NOTE FROM THE AUTHOR

I would like to thank the many freelance artists, staff, and studio assistants who have helped me in the studio over the years, as well as the editors and designers, past and present, at Scholastic, without whom this series would not have been possible. Details about the many contributors can be found in the individual books listed below.

Library of Congress Cataloging-in-Publication Data available

ISBN 978-0-545-83863-4

10 9 8 7 6 5 4 3 2 1   16 17 18 19 20
Printed in Malaysia 108
First edition, February 2016
Book design by Charles Kreloff and David Saylor

Dear Readers,

You are in for a challenge. A really, really big challenge! As I pored over the nine Can You See What I See? books, selected highlights from over 100 photographs, and wrote out the clues for my favorite hidden objects, I so enjoyed revisiting the creativity that has gone into this series for the past dozen or so years. The collection of thousands of diverse props, the building of sets and models, the arranging and photographing of those sets in my studio over all the years has resulted in the wonderland of real and imaginary worlds you now hold in your hands. From piles of buttons to retro robots, from shelves chock-full of tiny toys to far-flung scary castles, from dusty attics to shipwrecked treasure—all that and much more is here to delight and challenge with one simple question: Can you see what I see?

Good luck!

Walter Wick

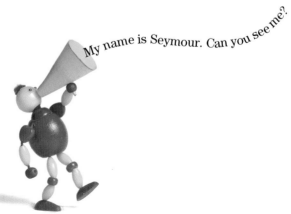

My name is Seymour. Can you see me?

 (Look for Seymour when you see this block.)

Can you see

√ a fox,

√ a deer,

√ 2 rabbits,

√ a windmill,

a black bird,

√ a well,

a pinecone,

√ an archer,

√ 4 horses,

and Puss in Boots?

Can you see

a ballerina,

a bell,

a skater,

a jack,

a king,

a blue shoe,

a panda,

a pear,

a fish,

and 2 flying penguins?

Can you see

√ a truck,

√ 3 clowns,

√ a yo-yo string,

√ a lion's tail,

√ a seal's ball,

a baby duck,

√ a silver car,

2 thimbles,

√ 3 monkeys,

and outstretched wings?

Can you see

2 rackets,

a lightning bolt,

3 playing cards,

√ a cardboard house,

√ 3 crayons,

a yellow duck,

a woman's shoe,

a big yellow star,

√ a night-light,

and planets on a shade?

Can you see

a silver heart,

a boat,

 a plane,

a chain,

a lock,

a jingle bell,

a telephone,

a rolling pin,

an eyeball ring,

and 8 strung beads?

Can you see

✓ 2 dice,

a dinosaur,

✓ a lobster,

a swan,

a car,

a crown,

a camel,

a gummy bear,

a smiley sun,

and a heart in a heart?

Can you see

√ a shovel,

√ a snail,

a bear,

an acorn,

a rolling pin,

a stovepipe,

√ a lantern,

√ 6 sweet hearts,

√ 2 tasty worms,

√ and a welcoming witch?

Can you see

a jar of honey,

a teapot spout,

a baby bottle,

a penguin,

a plane,

a clock,

a knight,

2 elephants,

windup teeth,

and lost truck wheels?

Can you see

2 dogs,

a bunny,

a teapot,

a domino,

a helmet,

2 hats,

a zipper,

the eye of a needle,

a blue button heart,

and a pretty pink bow?

Can you see

an anchor,

2 skulls,

6 palm trees,

a sun,

a moon,

a bell,

a crown,

2 keys,

3 birds,

and a whale's tail?

Can you see

a thimble,

an ox,

2 geese,

a feather,

a fan,

a pencil,

a purse,

a dartboard,

a dollar sign,

and a question mark?

Can you see

2 flowerpots,

an antler,

a bee,

3 acorns,

3 feathers,

a spider,

a squirrel,

a spotted stone,

a snake's rattle,

and a bee's home?

Can you see

a chicken,

a mouse,

a rabbit,

2 ducks,

a golf club,

a hammer,

a saw,

an iron,

a clothes hanger,

and a sturdy brick house?

Can you see

a skull,

a hat,

3 cats,

a comb,

a mitten,

a windmill,

a dinosaur,

a dolphin,

a dog,

and a thumbs-up?

Can you see

a mask,

an acorn,

a fish,

5 swans,

a rabbit,

a rat,

a pumpkin coach,

a violin,

a broken heart,

and a lost slipper?

Can you see

2 bats,

√ 3 baseballs,

a rocket,

a boat,

a starfish,

a ladybug,

scissors,

a magnet,

a red letter *J*,

and a gold star?

Can you see

3 bees,

a monkey,

a bat,

a key,

an elephant,

a white horse,

a leaping deer,

a perched parrot,

a bird in flight,

and a sheep at rest?

Can you see

a 3-piece fish,

a spotted fawn,

a hammer,

a house,

a swan,

a camel,

a toothpick,

a rolling pin,

a shoelace,

and a bunny's shirt?

Can you see

√ a sea horse,

a spider,

a ship,

2 shells,

a feather,

a dolphin,

a dog,

a castle,

a unicorn,

and an octopus?

Can you see

3 monkeys,

2 kangaroos,

a donkey,

a pony,

a pelican,

2 planes,

a train,

a moon face,

a blue sword,

and a yellow trunk?

Can you see

a camel,

a spring,

a hammer,

2 sneakers,

four 5's,

a sea horse,

a rocking chair,

3 playing cards,

a musical monkey,

and a magical moon?

Can you see

4 birds,

2 butterflies,

a snowman,

a snowflake,

a rainbow,

a letter *A*,

the number 9,

a girl watering,

a boy sweeping,

and binoculars?

Can you see

a swan,

2 dice,

a jack,

a checker,

a winged horse,

2 shiny suits,

a shovel,

a chess piece,

a lightning bolt,

and a water fountain?

Can you see

a yellow taxi,

a red bow tie,

3 boats,

4 planes,

a TV set,

a sun,

a king,

a shuttlecock,

a sleepy bunny,

and eyeball feet?

Can you see

3 pigs,

a red fire truck,

3 coins,

a camel,

2 bats,

5 flags,

a football,

an egg truck,

a spatula,

and a very scared man?

Can you see

a key,

a kettle,

a crank,

a glove,

a globe,

a watering can,

a mouse,

a magnet,

the number 12,

and an *H* for *hot*?

MOUSE VIEW

SIDE VIEW

Can you see

a cannon,

a cage,

a cat,

2 lions,

a pig,

a panda,

a bell,

a bunny,

a pencil point,

and a windmill?

Can you see

3 ears of corn,

a raccoon,

a cow,

2 clothespins,

a hatchet,

a ladder,

2 baskets,

a pitchfork,

a pear,

and a huffing, puffing wolf?

Can you see

a pinecone,

a stegosaurus,

a marble Earth,

a lobster claw,

a mask,

a motorcycle,

2 helmets,

a nut in a truck,

a knot in a string,

and a hungry bunny?

Can you see

a crystal ball,

a wizard,

a frog,

2 fish,

3 arrows,

a bridge,

3 birds,

a sun,

and a sailing ship?

Can you see

a light,

a kite,

a candle,

a cradle,

a spoon,

a moon,

a piano,

2 planes,

a fence,

and a flowerpot?

Can you see

a red thumbtack,

a rocking chair,

2 crayons,

a straw,

a dragon,

a mouse,

2 buttons,

a clothespin,

2 elephants,

and a television?

TOYLAND EXPRESS

Can you see

a football helmet,

a baseball bat,

a soccer ball,

2 bowling pins,

2 cats,

a dog,

a white pail,

a tennis racket,

a tricycle,

and 2 black hats?

Can you see

a stocking,

a sugarplum,

a teapot,

a fork,

a rose,

a rocket,

an airplane,

a baby carriage,

an ice cream cone,

and a candy train?

Can you see

an ostrich,

a zebra,

8 horses,

4 apes,

a pair of antlers,

3 polar bears,

a pumpkin,

dog food,

a spotted dog,

and a very bad cat?

Can you see

a dolphin,

2 sea horses,

a musical harp,

a lobster,

a bucket,

a plate,

a boat anchor,

4 starfish,

a mermaid,

and a circle of shells?

Can you see

a key,

a car,

a lock,

a flag,

a book,

a clock,

4 horses,

a red heart,

a bowling pin,

and a queen's empty hand?

Can you see

a whale,

a shark,

2 turtles,

a trumpet,

a clothespin,

a swordfish,

a sword,

a diamond,

a skull in the sand,

and a head on a ship?

Can you see

a candle,

a flashlight,

a thimble,

a phone,

a ruler,

a sled,

a dog,

a pig,

a duck,

and 3 trees?

Can you see

rain,

2 trees,

a faucet,

a whale,

2 fishing poles,

a parachute,

3 chairs,

a knife,

a cake,

and an open book?

Can you see

a clown,

a monkey,

a mouse,

an acorn,

a clock,

a candy cane,

a rooster,

a goose,

a steam train,

and a wishing well?

Can you see

a swan,

a chicken,

a goose,

a heart,

2 swords,

a moon,

a pumpkin,

a carriage,

2 crowns,

and 5 horses?

Can you see

a beach ball,

a soccer ball,

a gumball machine,

a bottle cap,

2 sand pails,

a dragon,

a monkey,

4 birds in flight,

a whale's tail,

and a distant ship?

Can you see

2 camels,

4 cars,

2 chickens,

a hot dog,

French fries,

a giraffe,

an owl,

2 arrows,

a castle,

and a king with heart?

Can you see

a newspaper,

a tub,

a jack-o'-lantern,

an apple,

a clock,

a strawberry,

a wagon,

a wrench,

a mouse,

and a rose?

Can you see

a rabbit,

a racket,

a whistle,

2 drummers,

a rocking horse,

a butterfly,

a turkey,

3 sheep,

2 giraffes,

and a sleepy mouse?

Can you see

a taxi,

a tow truck,

an airplane,

a steam train,

a motor scooter,

a milk truck,

a mail truck,

a checkered flag,

a stop sign,

and 2 exactly matching cars?

Can you see

an eel,

a lion,

a camel,

a serpent,

a shark,

a fork,

2 swans,

a rooster,

a pocket watch,

and an hourglass?

Can you see

a pig,

a propeller,

2 rabbits,

a tree,

a birdhouse,

3 elephants,

a rubber band,

a glue bottle,

2 keys,

and a monkey's tail?

Can you see

an open casket,

a telescope,

a turtle,

a frog,

a snake,

an octopus,

a knight,

3 keys,

witchy lightning,

and a screaming skull?

Can you see

a parrot,

a pirate flag,

a frying pan,

a blue umbrella,

a saw,

an ax,

an arrow,

2 clothespins,

crab legs,

and a keyhole?

Can you see

2 suns,

a man in the moon,

a trackball,

a key,

a guitar,

2 wings,

a rubber band,

2 lightning bolts,

antenna ears,

and a saltshaker nose?

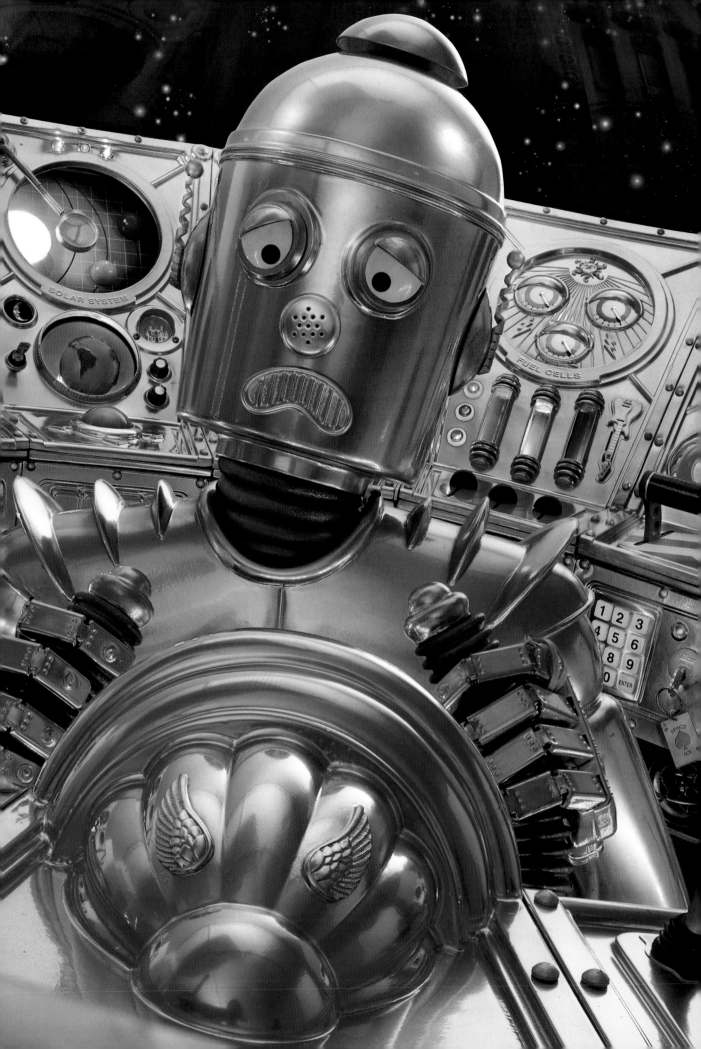

Can you see

a camel,

2 keys,

binoculars,

3 boats,

a mousetrap,

an umbrella,

a checkerboard,

a chair,

a glove,

and a horseshoe?

Can you see

3 bats,

a bell,

a lizard,

a monkey,

a lion,

a cat,

2 rats,

a crown,

a horseshoe,

and 2 scary skulls?

Can you see

a shovel,

a snowshoe,

a sled,

a cat,

owl eyes,

a carrot nose,

2 candy canes,

a gingerbread man,

a bird in flight,

and Santa's hat?

Can you see

a pony,

a pineapple,

a lobster plate,

a red thumbtack,

a silver bell,

a fishbowl,

a king's crown,

a sand clock,

a spyglass,

and 3 ships at sea?

Can you see

a dancer,

3 deer,

a pie,

a peppermint,

a snowman,

a spoon,

a wagon,

a train,

a white swan,

and a little blue angel?

Can you see

a flaming hood,

the number 4,

an open door,

2 ladders,

a nail,

a hex nut,

a horse head,

a cow,

2 ducks,

and a zebra truck?

Can you see

a die,

a domino,

a string,

a streetlight,

a lantern,

a candle,

a clock,

a knight,

4 giraffes,

and a queen of hearts?

Can you see

a flying saucer,

a football helmet,

a yellow funnel,

an oilcan,

2 bowling pins,

a whistle,

a top,

a key to wind,

a bucket for water,

and a grater for cheese?

Can you see

a clock,

a clothespin,

a spool,

a ladder,

2 boats,

a bridge,

a horse head,

a wagon wheel,

a sweet shoppe,

and 2 scary skull eyes?

Can you see

a king,

a ruler,

a spring toy,

2 planes,

a paper clip,

Saturn,

a sun,

2 dogs,

a blue bird,

and a locked heart?

Can you see

a frog,

a flute,

a feather,

2 roosters,

a zebra,

a xylophone,

a violin,

2 bunnies,

a blue flag,

and a broken rope?

Can you see

a sea horse,

an octopus,

2 rabbits,

lightning,

a moon,

a spider,

2 swans,

a starfish,

a hat feather,

and a bird that's wise?

XVI

THE TOWER

THE FOOL

XVIII

THE MOON

Can you see

a camel,

2 elephants,

3 giraffes,

a monkey,

2 dogs,

a lost ball,

2 umbrellas,

a trained lion,

a flying trapeze,

and a 6-piece band?

Can you see

a PUSH button,

a hand mixer,

a magnifying glass,

a bowling ball,

a bobby pin,

a barrette,

a heart,

a silver dime,

a saw,

and the sands of time?

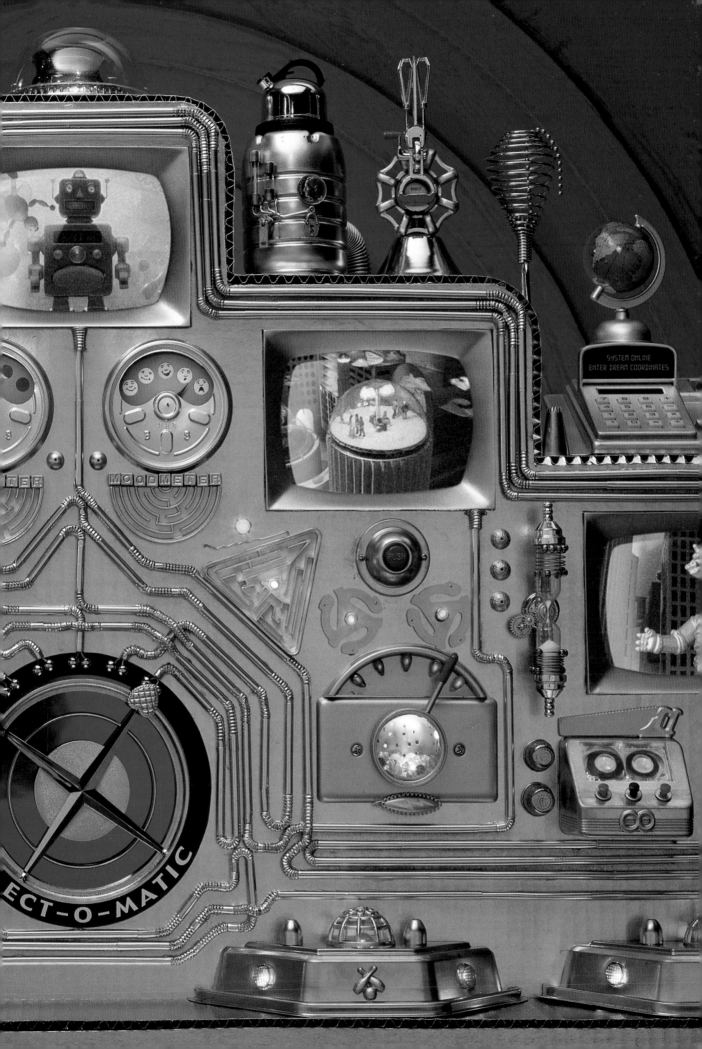

Can you see

a fire truck,

a red caboose,

a rocking horse,

a rubber duck,

a watering can,

an ice cream cone,

4 elephants,

a scorpion,

an airplane,

and a loose train wheel?

Can you see

a palm tree,

a pipe,

a crab,

a mouse,

a straw,

a door,

a die,

a skull,

3 ships,

and a shipwreck's treasure?

The Wreck of the *Bountiful*

Can you see

a dinosaur,

2 thimbles,

sunglasses,

a die,

a frog,

a bear,

a football,

2 rabbits,

a baseball bat,

and 4 birds?

Can you see

a bear,

a giraffe,

a Cyclops's skull,

a 2-headed lizard,

a skull bottle,

a spoon,

2 rabbit ears,

a grasshopper,

a hungry mouse,

and a skull-backed spider?

Can you see

3 crayons,

a caboose,

a whistle,

2 ducks,

4 bowling pins,

a football,

4 trees,

a bench,

a stop sign,

and 2 tasty cones?

Can you see

a jack-o'-lantern,

a barrel,

a bat,

a hammer,

a trash can,

a newspaper,

a crystal ball,

a long red nail,

an angry bear,

and a leaping frog?

Can you see

a clock,

a clothespin,

an oilcan,

a swim fin,

2 shuttlecocks,

a trophy,

a teacup,

2 spoons,

a mustard bottle,

and 14 flying cars?

Can you see

a pegasus,

a moon,

a waterfall,

2 owls,

a turtle,

a rabbit,

2 royal crowns,

a frisky cat,

a sleepy princess,

and a heart-shaped latch?

Can you see

3 letter *M*'s,

a strawberry,

a rocket,

a roller skate,

a bowling pin,

2 birds,

a jack,

a heart,

a flying eyeball,

and a 3-sided nose?

Can you see

a mouse,

a spring,

a hook,

a funnel,

a button,

a school bus,

a rubber band,

a glue bottle,

pencil shavings,

and a pencil?

Can you see

an elephant,

a kangaroo,

a giraffe,

a dinosaur,

a fire truck,

a rustic bridge,

a blue marble,

a baseball,

a crescent moon,

and the planet Earth?

Can You See What I See?

Also available are Can You See What I See?
board books and readers.

Find all the Can You See What I See? books and more
at www.scholastic.com/canyouseewhatisee/

Also Available

I Spy

Photographs by Walter Wick • Riddles by Jean Marzollo

Classics

Challengers

Also available are *I Spy A to Z, I Spy Spectacular, I Spy Sticker Book and Picture Riddles,* I Spy early readers, I Spy Little board books, and *I Spy Phonics Fun.*

Find all the I Spy books and more at www.scholastic.com/ispy/

Walter Wick is the photographer of the I Spy series and the creator of the Can You See What I See? series, with more than fifty-six million copies in print total. Both series have appeared on the *New York Times* bestseller list numerous times. He is the author and photographer of *A Drop of Water: A Book of Science and Wonder,* which won the Boston Globe/Horn Book Award for Nonfiction, was named a Notable Children's Book by the American Library Association, and was selected as an NCTE Orbis Pictus Honor Book and a CBC/NSTA Outstanding Science Trade Book for Students K–12. *Walter Wick's Optical Tricks,* a book of photographic illusions, was named a Best Illustrated Children's Book by the *New York Times Book Review,* was recognized as a Notable Children's Book by the American Library Association, and received many awards. Mr. Wick has been invited to numerous museums around the United States to exhibit his amazing photography and hand-built model sets for his search-and-find masterpieces. A graduate of Paier College of Art, Mr. Wick lives in Miami Beach, Florida, with his wife, Linda.